11/17

A TIMELINE OF

HELICOPTERS

by Tim Cooke

CAPSTONE PRESS
a capstone imprint

Edge Books are published by Capstone Press,
1710 Roe Crest Drive, North Mankato, Minnesota 56003
www.capstonepub.com

Published in 2018 by Capstone Publishing Ltd

Library of Congress Cataloging-in-Publication Data
Cataloging-in-publication information is on file with the Library of Congress.

ISBN: 978-1-5157-9198-0 (library binding)
ISBN: 978-1-5157-9204-8 (eBook PDF)

For Brown Bear Books Ltd:
Managing Editor: Tim Cooke
Designer: John Woolford
Editorial Director: Lindsey Lowe
Design Manager: Keith Davis
Children's Publisher: Anne O'Daly
Picture Manager: Sophie Mortimer
Production Director: Alastair Gourlay

Photo Credits
Front Cover: Alamy: Nir Ben-Yosef bl; Department of Defense: bc; Shutterstock: Guillermo Gonzalez br;
Robert Hunt Library: tc.
Interior: Alamy: Nir Ben-Yosef 16-17, Mike Fuchslocher 20-21t; Bell Helicopters: 28br; Department of Defense: 1,
9bc, 10-11t, 10-11b, 15tr, 17tr, 17br, 19tr, 20bc, 22-23, 25tr, 26-27, 27br, 28-29; Dreamstime: Vishwa Kiran 26br,
Zuboff 4; Getty Images: Scott Peterson/Hulton 23bl; Indian Air Force: 29br; National Archives: 8-9, 9bc, 9tr, 16br;
Robert Hunt Library: 5tr, 5cr, 5bl, 6-7t, 6-7b, 6bc, 7cr, 11tr, 12-13b, 13tr, 14bc, 21tr; San Diego Air and Space
Museum: 10bc; Shutterstock: cpaulfell 27tr, Paul Drabot 12-13t, Frontilt Photography 15bc, Guillermo Gonzalez
24-25t, 24-25b, Don Simonsen 12bc, Keith Tarrier 24bc, vaalaa 20-21b, VanderWolf Images 14-15, 22bc; Ukraine
Ministry of Defense: 18br; United Kingdom Ministry of Defence: 18-19, 19bc, 23tr, 29tr.
Artistic effects: Shutterstock

Brown Bear Books has made every attempt to contact the copyright holders.
If you have any information please contact licensing@brownbearbooks.co.uk

Printed in the USA
5607/AG/17

TABLE OF CONTENTS

ROTORCRAFT

A helicopter is a rotorcraft that uses spinning blades to lift it off the ground. A helicopter can take off and land vertically, so it can be used almost anywhere. Airplanes, in contrast, need runways to take off and land. Helicopters can also hover in one place.

The idea of the helicopter is very old. As long as 2,400 years ago, Chinese children made spinning tops by attaching **rotors** to a stick. When they spun the stick between their hands, the blades lifted the toy into the air. The French inventor Gustave Ponton d'Amécort made up the word "helicopter" in 1861. The first full-size helicopter for military use was not built until 1939. In the years since, helicopters have become essential to modern military forces.

EARLY DESIGN

In the 1480s Italian artist and inventor Leonardo da Vinci designed a spinning aircraft with a screwlike rotor. He never built his machine, but it has been recreated as a model by modern scientists. The machine would not have worked. The operator would not have been able to spin the rotor fast enough to make the machine fly.

EARLY AUTOGYROS

In 1923 the Spanish engineer Juan de la Cierva flew a rotorcraft called an autogyro. The machine resembled an airplane, but it also had rotor blades. The speed of the air turned the blades, which provided additional lift. This system allowed autogyros to fly slower than ordinary airplanes.

SIKORSKY VS-300

In 1939 Russian-born inventor Igor Sikorsky invented the first single-rotor helicopter. The VS-300 was the prototype of the first helicopter to go into production in the United States, the VS-316 (R-4).

GERMAN PIONEER

In Germany the Focke-Achgelis company had also invented a helicopter. The Fa 223 Drache had two rotors, one at the end of each of its winglike structures. In June 1942 **Allied forces** bombed the Focke-Achgelis factory. Only 20 Fa 223s were ever made.

rotor—a blade on an aircaft that spins around
Allied forces—belonging to the side that fought Germany and Japan in World War II; the main Allies were the United States, Great Britain, and the Soviet Union

FIRST HELICOPTERS

U.S. military forces began to use helicopters during World War II (1939–1945). These early military helicopters were used for casualty evacuation.

The first helicopter in U.S. military service was the two-seater Sikorsky R-4. Igor Sikorsky developed the aircraft from the VS-300. It went into service in 1943. In April 1944 a U.S. Army pilot carried out the first helicopter **combat rescue**. A U.S. airplane had crashed in the jungle in the south Asian country of Burma, where the Allies were fighting the Japanese. The helicopter rescued four men, flying them to safety over the mountains.

MAIN ROTOR
had three blades powered by a piston engine.

FULLY ENCLOSED COCKPIT
had dual controls for the two-man crew.

TIMELINE

1936
TWIN-ROTOR
The Germans build the first aircraft with two rotors, the Focke-Wulf Fw 61.

1944
CANCELLED XR-1
The U.S. Amy cancels its contract for the XR-1, an early form of rotorcraft.

SPECIFICATIONS

SIKORSKY R-4

Weight: 2,098 pounds (952 kilograms)
Length: 33 feet 8 inches (10.2 meters)
Crew: 2
Rotor diameter: 38 feet (11.5 meters)
Main armament: none
Top speed: 75 miles (120 kilometers) per hour

POWER PEOPLE

IGOR SIKORSKY

In 1913 Russian-born engineer Igor Sikorsky (1889–1972) invented the first four-engined airplane. He later worked in Paris. Sikorsky moved to the United States in 1919. He created his own company to develop the first helicopter. He invented the VS-300 in 1939.

FRAME
of steel tubes is covered by canvas, apart from at the tail.

1944

COMBAT RESCUE

A U.S. Sikorsky R-4 carries out the first helicopter combat rescue in the jungles of Burma.

1945

FIRST MEDEVAC

U.S. pilots use the R-4 to airlift casualties from the front line to the hospital.

casualty—someone injured or killed in a war
combat rescue—the rescue of someone from a battlefield

7

MEDEVAC

After World War II, the Sikorsky company continued to develop helicopters. Rotorcraft were widely used in the next military conflict, the Korean War (1950–1953).

U.S. forces in Korea fought with South Korea and several other countries against **communist** North Korea and China. Helicopters such as the Sikorsky H-5 and HO3S-1 were used to rescue U.S. pilots who had been shot down behind enemy lines. They were also used for medical evacuation, or medevac. They flew injured soldiers from the **front line** to field hospitals, known as Mobile Army Surgical Hospitals (MASH). The helicopters could tip over quite easily, so pilots had to carry heavy iron bars to try to keep them stable.

COMPARTMENT behind the pilot provides seating for passengers.

NOSEWHEEL gives more stability when landing.

TIMELINE

1946
BELL 47
The U.S. firm Bell Helicopter introduces the Bell 47, which is used by both military forces and civilian operators.

1947
BELL H-13 SIOUX
Bell introduces a new lightweight observation helicopter. The H-13 is used by both U.S. and British military forces.

SPECIFICATIONS

SIKORSKY HO3S-1

Weight: 3,780 pounds
(1,718 kilograms)
Length: 57 feet 1 inch (17.4 meters)
Crew: 1 pilot, 3 passengers
Main rotor blades: 3
Rotor diameter: 48 feet
(14.63 meters)
Main armament: none
Top speed: 106 miles (171 kilometers)
per hour

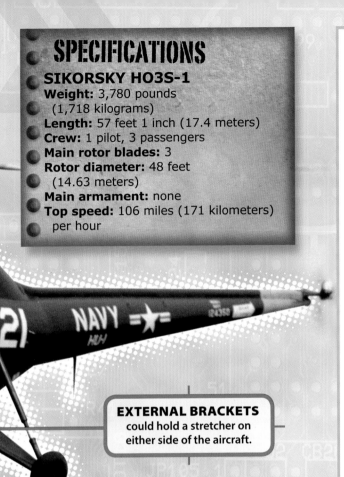

EXTERNAL BRACKETS
could hold a stretcher on
either side of the aircraft.

IN ACTION

MASH IN KOREA

In wartime, the faster
wounded soldiers reach the
hospital, the more chance
they have of survival. In
Korea, the U.S. Army set up
MASH, or surgical hospitals,
in tents close to the front
lines. Helicopters such as
the Sikorsky H-5, HO3S-1,
and the H-19 Chickasaw
picked up wounded men
and flew them to the MASH.

1950

SIKORSKY H-5

Sikorsky introduces
the H-5, which can
carry heavier loads
and fly quicker and
farther than the R-4.

1950

KOREA MEDEVAC

Helicopters are
widely used to
evacuate injured
soldiers from the front
line in the Korean War.

communist—based on a political system in which the state controls all economic activity
front line—the place in a war where opposing forces are closest to one another

AIRMOBILE TACTICS

In the late 1950s, French forces began to arm their helicopters. This was a step toward airmobile warfare. This was warfare based on carrying out assaults by helicopter.

The French were fighting rebels in their colony in Algeria in the Algerian War (1954–1962). They put machine gunners on the stretcher carriers outside their helicopters. Machine guns, rockets, and bombs were added to other helicopters. They used these helicopter gunships to attack targets on the ground. Other helicopters, such as the Piasecki CH-21, landed assault troops to attack the same targets. The helicopter had an unusual shape. Its back end tilted upward so the two rotors could not hit one another. U.S. pilots called the CH-21 the "flying banana."

TANDEM ROTORS rotated in opposite directions.

BODY had room for 22 armed soldiers or 12 casualties on stretchers.

TIMELINE

1951
TURBINE HELICOPTER
The Kaman HTK is the first helicopter to use a turbine engine rather than a piston engine.

1954
H-34 CHOCTAW
Sikorsky introduces the H-34, which is designed to be flown from aircraft carriers for fighting against submarines.

SPECIFICATIONS

PIASECKI CH-21 SHAWNEE
Weight: 8,950 pounds
   (4,058 kilograms)
Length: 52 feet 6 inches (16.01 meters)
Crew: 3–5
Rotor diameter: 44 feet
   (13.41 meters)
Main armament: 2 M60 machine guns
Top speed: 127 miles (204 kilometers)
   per hour

IN ACTION

ALGERIAN WAR

The French set up a colony in Algeria in North Africa in 1830. In 1954 **nationalists** rebelled against French rule. The French used helicopters to move their troops rapidly to fight them. They also attacked rebel positions from the air using helicopter gunships. Many Fench people turned against the war, however. In 1962 the French granted Algeria independence.

UPWARD BEND
of the fuselage made sure the rotor blades did not clash.

1954
ALGERIAN WAR
French forces use helicopters to fight nationalist rebels in their colony in the Algerian War.

1954
DISTANCE FLIGHT
A CH-21 Shawnee makes a nonstop flight across the United States.

tactic—a planned method to achieve victory in a military battle
nationalist—someone who believes their country should govern itself

AERIAL CAVALRY

Helicopters were the main U.S. aircraft of the Vietnam War (1955–1975). They were the only way for soldiers and Marines to reach remote areas of Vietnam where there were few roads.

> **TWO-BLADED** rotor can be folded to take up less storage space.

There were few set battles in the war. U.S. forces made patrols into the Vietnamese countryside. They were looking for enemy soldiers hiding among the local population. Helicopters flew patrols into position and picked them up after their mission. In some ways, the helicopters performed the role of **cavalry** by making rapid raids to locate the enemy. The most common helicopter of the war was the Bell UH-1. Soldiers nicknamed it the Huey. U.S. forces used about 7,000 Hueys during the Vietnam War.

TIMELINE

1957

ALOUETTE II
French forces in Algeria begin to arm their Alouette II helicopters.

1959

UH-1 HUEY
Bell introduces the UH-1 Iroquois, known as the Huey. The Huey becomes one of the most widely used military helicopters in the world.

SPECIFICATIONS

BELL UH-1 HUEY

Weight: 5,215 pounds
  (2,365 kilograms)
Length: 57 feet 1 inch (17.4 meters)
Crew: 1–4
Rotor diameter: 48 feet
  (14.63 meters)
Main armament: 2 machine guns
  or 2 rocket pods
Top speed: 135 miles
  (217 kilometers) per hour

EYEWITNESS

DOORS
can be removed
to enable weapons to
be mounted inside
the helicopter.

SKID TUBES
enable the Huey to land
on uneven ground.

> I remember choppers [helicopters] rising straight out of small cleared jungle spaces or wobbling down onto city rooftops. Cartons of rations and ammunition thrown off, dead and wounded loaded on. Sometimes there were so many helicopters that you could touch down at five or six places a day, look around, and catch the next one out. Flying over the jungle was almost pure pleasure. Doing it on foot was almost all pain.

Michael Herr, U.S. war correspondent, Vietnam War

1960

ALOUETTE III
French forces in Algeria use a new, larger version of the Alouette to evacuate casualties.

1961

WAR IN VIETNAM
U.S. helicopters arrive in Vietnam to support South Vietnamese troops fighting communist North Vietnam.

cavalry—soldiers on horseback used throughout history for patrols and rapid attacks on the enemy

HEAVY TRANSPORTATION

As well as carrying soldiers and carrying weapons, helicopters had a growing role in transporting military supplies.

In the late 1950s, the U.S. Army began to develop a new helicopter that could carry heavy loads. The machine was eventually named the Chinook CH-47. The Chinook had two sets of rotors that helped it to remain stable when it lifted heavy loads off the ground. A ramp at the tail end allowed vehicles or large groups of soldiers to be carried inside the body of the helicopter. There were also three strong hooks beneath the aircraft. They were used to lift **artillery** guns and vehicles in heavy slings.

CARGO HOOKS beneath the helicopter can lift vehicles and cargo nets.

TIMELINE

1962
CH-47 CHINOOK
The CH-47 Chinook heavy transportation helicopter is introduced. It is still in service today.

1962
CH-46 SEA KNIGHT
The U.S. Marine Corps introduces the twin-rotored CH-46 Sea Knight for transportation and close air support.

CH-47 CHINOOK
Weight: 24,578 pounds
  (11,148 kilograms)
Length: 98 feet 10 inches
  (30.1 meters)
Crew: 3
Rotor diameter: 60 feet
  (18.3 meters)
Main armament: 3 machine guns
Top speed: 196 miles
  (315 kilometers) per hour

IN ACTION

TWO ROTORS can be controlled separately to fit the weight distribution of the load.

WIDE RAMP at the back gives easy acces for up to 55 soldiers or 24 cargo pallets.

AFGHANISTAN

U.S. forces began fighting Taliban rebels in Afghanistan in 2001. The Chinook was useful because it flew better at high **altitude** in the mountains of Afghanistan than smaller helicopters. It could also carry more soldiers and supplies to U.S. **firebases**. Firebases were set up in territory where the enemy might be active. Soldiers made patrols in the area then returned to the bases for safety.

1966 »»

OH-6 CAYUSE
U.S. forces in Vietnam use the Hughes OH-6 Cayuse as a light observation helicopter.

1966

SEA STALLION
The U.S. Marines order the Sea Stallion, a powerful, twin-rotor heavy transportation helicopter.

artillery—large guns such as cannons
altitude—height above sea level
firebase—a base defended by heavy guns such as cannons

ATTACK HELICOPTERS

By the late 1960s, helicopters were becoming increasingly strongly armed. They had short stub wings to carry machine guns, and multiple missiles and rockets for striking targets on the ground.

PLEXIGLASS canopy gives wide view for pilot and copilot-gunner.

Attack helicopters such as the AH-1 Cobra could provide support for troops during an advance. The helicopters acted like a form of aerial artillery. They flew close to the ground, so they could fire at enemy forces without endangering friendly troops. Some helicopters also carried anti-tank missiles. They destroyed enemy tanks and other armor, as well as enemy bases. Attack helicopters were more streamlined than earlier helicopters. They flew fast to reduce the risk of being shot down.

TIMELINE

1967
LONG-RANGE
U.S. forces introduce the MH-53 Pave Low for long-range missions to find and destroy enemy forces.

1967
ATTACK WEAPON
The Bell AH-1 Cobra is introduced by U.S. forces as an attack helicopter in Vietnam.

SPECIFICATIONS

BELL AH-1 COBRA

Weight: 5,810 pounds
   (2,630 kilograms)
Length: 53 feet (16.2 meters)
Crew: 2
Rotor diameter: 44 feet
   (13.4 meters)
Main armament: 2 miniguns,
   up to 19 rockets, 20mm cannon
Top speed: 171 miles
   (277 kilometers) per hour

INSIDE OUT

MISSILES AND GUNS

As helicopters have become more heavily armed, the arrangement of weapons has become more standard. The nose carries a machine gun and possibly a grenade launcher. The stub wings contain four **hardpoints**. These fixtures are used for attaching missiles, which can strike targets on the ground or in the air. The hardpoints also contain tubes that carry multiple rockets of various sizes.

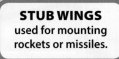

STUB WINGS used for mounting rockets or missiles.

TURRET beneath nose contains miniguns and grenade launcher.

1968 ▶▶▶

HUEY UPGRADE

Bell releases an upgraded UH-1, with increased lifting capacity. It is known as the Huey Tug.

1969 ▶▶▶

OH-58 KIOWA

The U.S. Army introduces the OH-58 Kiowa for observation and fire support. The OH-58 has been in continuous use since the 1970s.

hardpoint—a place on an aircraft designed to carry a load

SEABORNE HELICOPTERS

Helicopters are useful in naval warfare. They can take off and land from the decks of warships. That makes them useful weapons.

Navies first used helicopters for search-and-rescue missions. The helicopters carried **winches** to pull sailors and airmen from the ocean. Later naval helicopters also acted as attack helicopters. They could also resupply ships at sea with supplies, ammunition, or fuel. Helicopters such as the Sea King flew from the decks of aircraft carriers. Modern ships are built with a flat **helipad** so that they can carry one or two smaller helicopters on board.

HOIST is used to rescue people from the sea or from the decks of ships.

DOORWAY is fitted with mounts for machine guns.

TIMELINE

1969
ROYAL NAVY
The Westland Sea King HAS.1 becomes the major naval helicopter of Britain's Royal Navy.

1972
SOVIET HIND
The Mi-24 Hind becomes the main attack helicopter of the Soviet Union and its communist allies.

SPECIFICATIONS

SEA KING HAS.5

Weight: 14,051 pounds
(6,387 kilograms)

Length: 55 feet 10 inches
(17.02 meters)

Crew: 2–4

Rotor diameter: 62 feet
(18.90 meters)

Main armament: 4 torpedoes or
depth charges

Top speed: 129 miles (208 kilometers)
per hour

INSIDE OUT

RESCUE SWIMMERS

Helicopters often fly very close to the surface of the sea. They drop rescue swimmers through the large open door. The swimmers rescue people in the water. The helicopter has systems that warn if the aircraft is too close to the water. In rough seas, rescue swimmers might have to jump from up to 40 feet (12.2 meters) above the water. They use large exterior winches to raise casualties to the helicopter.

BOAT HULL
allows the helicopter to land on water.

1978

WESTLAND LYNX
The British introduce the Lynx. It is the first helicopter capable of flying loops and rolls.

1979

BLACK HAWK
The Black Hawk becomes the main utility helicopter of the U.S. Army, replacing the Bell UH-1 Huey.

winch—a lifting device in which a cable winds around a revolving drum

helipad—a small area for helicopters to take off and land

SPECIAL FORCES

Since the Vietnam War, armies have made increasing use of special forces. Helicopters can transport forces such as the Green Berets or Navy SEALs to missions deep inside hostile territory.

A helicopter such as the UH-60 Black Hawk can carry a team of up to 11 soldiers. It can fly low to avoid being detected on enemy radar. A variation of the Black Hawk used by airborne special operations has been adapted so its rotors make less noise. It uses **stealth** technology to reduce its profile on radar. The Black Hawk is also heavily armed and carries two gunners in case it comes under fire.

SIDE MOUNTINGS
used for machine guns.

BUNDESHE

WINDOWS
allow gunners to seek
targets and fire handguns.

TIMELINE

1980

SPECIAL OPS
The MH-6 Little Bird enters service among U.S. special forces. Because of its shape, it is nicknamed the "killer egg."

1982

KAMOV KA-27
The Soviet Union introduces the Kamov Ka-27 naval helicopter for anti-submarine warfare.

SPECIFICATIONS

UH-60 BLACK HAWK
Weight: 10,624 pounds
(4,819 kilograms)
Length: 64 feet 10 inches
(19.76 meters)
Crew: 2 pilots, 2 gunners
Rotor diameter: 53 feet 8 inches
(16.36 meters)
Main armament: 6 machine guns,
plus rockets, missiles, and bombs
Top speed: 183 miles
(294 kilometers) per hour

IN ACTION

ABBOTTABAD
On a dark night in May 2011 two Black Hawk helicopters carried Navy SEALs to Abbottabad in Pakistan. The SEALs had learned that the wanted terrorist Osama bin Laden was hiding there. One of the Black Hawks crash landed in bin Laden's compound. The SEALs survived. They found and killed bin Laden. Before they left, they blew up the crashed helicopter. They did not want anyone to learn about its technology.

TANKS
on stub wings at top of helicopter carry extra fuel.

1982
PAVE HAWK
U.S. forces introduce the HH-60 Pave Hawk, which is used to transport special forces for missions.

1984
SEAHAWK
The U.S. Navy introduces the SH-60 Seahawk, a variation of the Black Hawk used for naval and anti-submarine warfare.

special forces—armed units that undertake secret operations against terrorists
stealth—using advanced design and technology to avoid being detected

HELICOPTER GUNSHIPS

By the 1990s attack helicopters were more heavily armed than ever before. They carried weapons with great destructive power. These aircraft became known as helicopter gunships.

U.S. helicopter gunships fired the first shots of the Gulf War (1991). The aircraft were mainly AH-64 Apaches. They used missiles to destroy Iraqi radar facilities and missile bases before ground troops advanced. France and Britain also used helicopter gunships such as the Eurocopter Tiger to protect civilians during a civil war in Libya in 2011. The gunships destroyed Libyan tanks and military checkpoints set up by forces supporting the **dictator**, Muammar Gaddafi.

RADAR
mounted above rotor blades gives information to weapons systems.

HEAVY GUN
beneath cockpit can be aimed in any direction.

TIMELINE

1986
APACHE
The American AH-64 Apache goes into service. It becomes the main strike helicopter of many nations.

1986
SUPER COBRA
The Bell AH-1W SuperCobra enters service. It becomes the main attack helicopter of the U.S. Marine Corps.

SPECIFICATIONS

AH-64 APACHE
Weight: 11,387 pounds
(5,165 kilograms)
Length: 58 feet 2 inches
(17.73 meters)
Crew: 2
Rotor diameter: 48 feet
(14.63 meters)
Main armament:
1 chaingun, plus 4
hardpoints for rockets
and missiles
Top speed: 182 miles
(293 kilometers) per hour

EYEWITNESS

" We are actually fairly well protected. I'm armored below myself, behind me, on my side, and then I'll wear a protected vest. The aircraft itself, the Black Hawk, is just an amazing machine. They've gotten shot up and shot up and shot up and they'll just keep flying. "

Drew David Larson, pilot, 82nd Medical Company, U.S. Army, Iraq

HELLFIRE missiles are carried on weapons pylons.

HYDRA-70 rocket systems carry up to 19 rockets in tube launchers.

1993

BLACK HAWK DOWN
A U.S. Black Hawk is shot down by rebel forces in Mogadishu during a peacekeeping operation in Somalia.

1994

CHINESE HELICOPTER
The Chinese introduce the Harbin Z-9 as an armed helicopter. It is adapted from a civilian helicopter with hardpoints for missiles and rockets.

dictator—a ruler who imposes his will on his people

ANTI-SUBMARINE WARFARE

As technology has developed, naval helicopters have become an important weapon in submarine warfare. They can detect enemy submarines deep beneath the ocean.

Modern submarines can stay submerged for months at a time. They are difficult to detect. Helicopters such as the MH-60R carry **sonar** units that they lower into the water on a winch. Sonar detects any underwater sounds, including the sound of a submarine's engines. Helicopter sonar is more sensitive than ship-based sonar, which can suffer from interference from the ship's own engines. Helicopters can also search larger areas for submarine activity than ships, because they travel more quickly.

DIPPING SONAR
carried on long winch beneath the helicopter.

TIMELINE

2000

JAPANESE FIRST
Japanese forces begin to fly the first ever Japanese military helicopter. The Kawasaki OH-1 is a scout helicopter.

2003

EUROCOPTER
European nations cooperate to develop the Eurocopter Tiger, an attack helicopter that uses stealth technology.

SPECIFICATIONS

MH-60R SEAHAWK
Weight: 15,200 pounds
(6,895 kilograms)
Length: 64 feet 8 inches
(19.75 meters)
Crew: 3–4
Rotor diameter: 53 feet 8 inches
(16.35 meters)
Main armament: 3 torpedoes,
1 machine gun, up to 8 missiles
Top speed: 168 miles
(270 kilometers) per hour

INSIDE OUT

USING SONAR
Anti-submarine helicopters carry small sonar **buoys** that they scatter over a large area of the ocean. Each buoy carries a sonar that sinks beneath the water. The transmitter on the surface sends signals to the helicopter if it detects any sound. Helicopters also lower their own sonar into the ocean on long cables.

SIDE PANEL
carries sonar buoys to drop into the ocean.

RADAR SENSORS
are in pod on nose of aircraft.

2007
TILTROTOR
The U.S. Marine Corps introduces the MV-22 Osprey, its first tiltrotor aicraft.

2008
CANCELLATION
The U.S. Army cancels its contract for the ARH-70 Osprey observation helicopter because of rising costs.

sonar—a device that locates objects underwater by listening for sounds

buoy—a device that floats in a fixed place

TILTROTOR CRAFT

Since the first helicopters flew, designers have tried to come up with a new kind of aircraft. Ideally it would take off and land vertically, like a helicopter, but it would fly as fast as an airplane.

Designers came up with a tiltrotor. The aircraft's propellers are housed in units at the end of the wings. The blades rotate horizontally for takeoff and landing, like the rotors of a helicopter. Once the tiltrotor is in the air, the propeller units gradually twist until the blades are rotating vertically. The propellers thrust the tiltrotor through the air like airplane propellers. That made tiltrotors such as the V-22 Ospreys far quicker than ordinary helicopters. However, they are still able to take off and land vertically and hover.

PIVOTS
turn propeller pods at the end of wings.

LOADING RAMP
at the rear of the aircraft holds up to 24 soldiers.

TIMELINE

2009
U.S. AIR FORCE
The U.S. Air Force introduces its first tiltrotor aircraft, the CV-22 Osprey.

2010
LIGHT HELICOPTER
The Indian Army begins testing the HAL Light Combat Helicopter, designed to fly at high altitudes in India's mountains.

SPECIFICATIONS

MV-22 OSPREY
Weight: 33,140 pounds
(15,032 kilograms)
Length: 57 feet 4 inches (17.5 meters)
Crew: 4
Rotor diameter: 38 feet (11.6 meters)
Main armament: 1 machine gun,
1 minigun
Top speed: 351 miles (565 kilometers)
per hour

INSIDE OUT

TILTROTORS

The idea of a tiltrotor aircraft has always appealed to military commanders. Tiltrotors are far quicker through the air than normal helicopters. However, they can still take off and land vertically. This means they do not need special **air strip** to operate.
The aircraft can also hover above a fixed position, so it can provide support for ground troops operating immediately below.

WINDOW
lets one of two gunners
fire automatic weapons.

PROBE
allows midair refueling
to increase range.

2012

NEW HARBIN
The Chinese update
the Harbin Z-9 to
create the Z-19
reconnaissance and
attack helicopter.

2015

BIGGEST EVER
The CH-53K King Stallion
makes its first flight.
It is developed for the
U.S. Marine Corps and
will be the largest heavy
military helicopter.

air strip—a simple runway without hangars or other buildings

NEW GENERATION

Helicopters continue to become bigger, faster, and better armed. They will likely be at the heart of conflicts against terrorist groups and rebels around the world.

The U.S. Marine Corps is developing the largest helicopter ever to enter U.S. military service. The CH-53K King Stallion will be able to carry up to 55 troops. It will carry loads nearly twice as heavy as any other cargo helicopter. Its cockpit is equipped with electronic controls. A computer will interpret the pilot's commands and fly the helicopter accordingly to get the best performance. The aircraft also carries three machine guns, so it will be able to defend itself if necessary.

MAIN ROTOR has seven blades to increase lifting capacity.

ENGINES are mounted on the outside of helicopter body.

INTO THE FUTURE

BELL V-280 VALOR
Bell is developing a new tiltrotor craft for the US Army. The Bell V-280 will be twice as fast as any existing helicopter, and will have twice the range. It will have computer systems that give the crew real-time updates on action on the battlefield. This will enable it to provide support.

SPECIFICATIONS

CH-53K KING STALLION
Weight: 33,226 pounds
(15,071 kilograms)
Length: 99 feet (30.2 meters)
Crew: 5
Rotor diameter: 79 feet (24 meters)
Main armament: 3 machine guns
Cruise speed: 196 miles
(315 kilometers) per hour

FUTURE VERTICAL LIFT PROGRAM

The U.S. Army calls its helicopter development program Future Vertical Lift (FVL). It believes FVL will be essential in future wars. The program aims to fill gaps in the ability of the U.S. helicopter fleet. Planners want helicopters that can fly higher, where the air is thinner. They want aircraft that can carry more equipment such as radar and weapons systems. They also think helicopters should have more flexible uses in battlezones, and have a longer range than existing helicopters.

LANDING GEAR
retracts in flight to
reduce air resistance.

LIGHT COMBAT

The Indian Army is developing a new Light Combat Helicopter (LCH). It needs to be able to fly in thin air at high altitudes in India's mountains. It will carry antipersonnel and antiartillery weapons.

GLOSSARY

air strip (AYR STRIP)—a simple runway without hangars or other buildings

Allied forces (AL-lyd FORSS-uhs)—belonging to the side that fought Germany and Japan in World War II; the main Allies were the United States, Great Britain, and the Soviet Union

altitude (AL-ti-tood)—height above sea level

artillery (ar-TIL-uh-ree)—large guns such as cannons

buoy (BOO-ee)—a device that floats in a fixed place

casualty (KAZH-oo-uhl-tee)—someone injured or killed in a war

cavalry (CAV-ul-ree)—soldiers on horseback used throughout history for patrols and rapid attacks on the enemy

combat rescue (KOM-bat RES-kyoo)—the rescue of someone from a battlefield

communist (COM-yew-nist)—based on a political system in which the state controls all economic activity

dictator (DIK-tay-tuhr)—a ruler who imposes his will on his people

firebase—a base defended by heavy guns such as cannons

front line (FRUHNT LYN)—the place in a war where opposing forces are closest to one another

hardpoint (HARD-poynt)—a place on an aircraft meant to carry a load

helipad (HEL-uh-pad)—a small area for helicopters to take off and land

nationalist (NASH-uh-nuhl-ist)—a person who believes their country should govern itself

rotor (ROH-tur)—a blade on an aircaft that spins around

sling (SLING)—a strap or belt that support hanging weights

sonar (SO-nar)—a device that locates objects underwater by listening for sounds

special forces (SPESH-ul FOR-sez)—armed units that undertake secret missions against terrorists

stealth (STELTH)—using advanced design and technology to avoid being detected

tactic (TAC-tic)—a planned method to achieve victory in a battle

winch (WINCH)—a lifting device in which a cable winds around a revolving drum

READ MORE

Harasymiw, Mark. *Military Helicopters*. Military Machines. New York: Gareth Stevens, 2013.

Kiland, Taylor Baldwin, and Glen Bledsoe. *Military Helicopters*. Military Engineering in Action. Berkeley Heights, NJ: Enslow Publishing, 2015.

Nagelhout, Ryan. *Military Helicopters*. Mighty Military Machines. New York: Gareth Stevens Publishing, 2015.

INTERNET SITES

Use FactHound to find Internet sites related to this book.

Visit www.facthound.com

Just type in 9781515791980 and go.

Super-cool stuff! Check out projects, games and lots more at
www.capstonekids.com

INDEX